Quit smoking for good!

Andrew McCoig
Dr Alex Bobak

Quit smoking for good!
First published – December 2006
Reprinted – June 2007

Published by
CSF Medical Communications Ltd
Suite 119, Eagle Tower
Montpellier Drive, Cheltenham, GL50 1TA, UK
T +44 (0)1242 223890 F +44 (0)1242 243406
enquiries@thesimpleguides.com
www.thesimpleguides.com

We are always interested in hearing from anyone
who has anything to add to our Simple Guides.
Please send your comments to *editor@thesimpleguides.com*

Author Andrew McCoig
Medical Editor Dr Alex Bobak
Science Editor Dr Scott Chambers
Layout Jamie McCansh and Julie Smith
Operations Julia Savory
Publisher Stephen l'Anson

© CSF Medical Communications Ltd 2006, 2007

All rights reserved

ISBN-10: 1-905466-28-5
ISBN-13: 978-190546-628-3

The contents of this Simple Guide should not be treated as a substitute for the medical advice of your own doctor or any other healthcare professional. You are strongly urged to consult your doctor before taking, stopping or changing any of the products or lifestyle recommendations referred to in this book or any other medication that has been prescribed or recommended by your doctor. Whilst every effort has been made to ensure the accuracy of the information at the date of publication, CSF Medical Communications Ltd and The Patients Association accept no responsibility for any errors or omissions or for any consequences arising from anything included in or excluded from this Simple Guide nor for the contents of any external internet site or other information source listed and do not endorse any commercial products or services mentioned.

Printed in Great Britain.

Contents

Preface	v
Introduction	ix
Nicotine – cause and effect	**1**
The first cigarette of the day	2
So what else is going on?	5
Why do I seem to feel 'better' after I've lit up?	6
But smoking keeps me thin…	8
… and anyway, food isn't all that important to me	10
Am I really addicted… surely it's just a habit that I could break at anytime?	12
What about the financial aspects of smoking?	16
Risks versus benefits	**21**
What is dangerous in cigarette smoke?	26
Not everyone who smokes gets cancer so what other diseases could I get?	28
I'm nearly convinced, but my granddad lived till he was 85 and smoked all his life. So why can't I?	30
I've heard smoking can affect your skin and the way you look – is this right?	31
So you're saying that everything about me will improve?	34
What about passive smoking?	35
Time for action	**37**
Dump the denial!	38
Get help!	41
Make the call – it's FREE!	42
Professional support	44

You're on your way... now stick with it!	46
Reaching for the new you!	50
Positive action points	51
Don't make excuses	52
Keep busy	54
Clean away those awful smells	54
Persuade someone to quit with you	54
Do your sums!	56

Stop smoking products	**59**
What's available?	60
Nicotine replacement therapy	60
What else is available that can help me quit?	79
Drug therapy for quitting	80

Stay stopped!	**87**
You'll now feel great. Enjoy the new you!	89
Top 20 tips to help you stay stopped	90

Simple extras	**95**
What happens normally?	96
What do our lungs normally do?	96
Why is oxygen and carbon dioxide exchange important?	98
Your circulatory system	98
What happens when we smoke?	101
Shared experiences	104
Further reading	108
Useful contacts	108
Your rights	111
Simple Guides questionnaire	115

PREFACE

ANDREW MCCOIG

For a smoker to be able to quit smoking successfully, they need to take a series of positive steps. By purchasing and reading this Simple Guide you've already taken the first of these positive steps towards quitting smoking for good! Hopefully, this should be the start of a process that will change your life forever and for the better.

I am a practising community pharmacist who has helped hundreds of smokers since nicotine replacement therapy (NRT) was first introduced in the early 1990s. To date, I have enrolled more than 700 smokers into my pharmacy's stop smoking programme. Although not all of these people have quit, a significant percentage have been very successful and have remained smoke free and have rid themselves of the scourge and the expense of tobacco, hopefully for the remainder of their now extended lives.

A year after the 1997 general election, the Government published a lengthy White Paper entitled *Smoking Kills*. This set out a strategic policy for reducing smoking across the UK and established a series of targets for individual NHS agencies and other relevant organisations. Following on from the White Paper, in 2002 the NHS introduced a scheme that allowed any smoker in England to access a free counselling service, which was linked to the supply of NRT and another evidenced-based treatment called Zyban®.

Many scientific papers have been published which establish, beyond doubt, that NRT and Zyban achieve the most success when they are backed up with a structured support and counselling service. It has been well documented that smokers who purchase NRT over the counter without such support are far less likely to succeed with their quit attempt than those who have access to a full supporting service linked to specifically agreed treatment plans.

In this Simple Guide, I will explain to you:

- why you're addicted to nicotine
- how you can overcome your addiction by taking one simple step at a time
- how you can remain a non-smoker for the rest of your life.

At the end of this Simple Guide I have also given you 20 top tips (think of these as a replacement for your favourite 20 filter tips!) on how to ensure that you can quit smoking for good (page 90)! You'll also be able to read about some real life experiences from smokers who have tried and have been successful in their quest to kick the habit (page 104).

Dumping an addiction is not, and never will be, easy. Accepting this simple and inalienable fact is the first part of the challenge that you will face. At the present time, being addicted to nicotine is not illegal, though even the majority of smokers consider it to be a highly undesirable habit and something they often wish they'd never started. The knowledge you will gain from reading this Simple Guide together with your own personal commitment and determination to follow my advice will help you to end this deadly habit and return to a normal and healthier lifestyle that the majority of non-smokers currently enjoy as a basic human right.

You can do it!

INTRODUCTION

"Have you not reason then to be ashamed and to forbear this filthy novelty, so basely grounded, so foolishly received and so grossly mistaken in the right use thereof."
James I, King of England 1604

Just 40 years ago smoking was accepted as a socially acceptable and even a desirable activity. It was widely advertised, pushed at us incessantly and portrayed on TV and in the cinema as an everyday, everybody does it activity. It seemed that smoking would even make us sexy without any apparent adverse effects. However, Humphrey Bogart, John Wayne, Audrey Hepburn, George Harrison and Princess Margaret have all been victims of death by smoking.

In recent times, smoking has been more correctly portrayed as an addiction. Smokers are at best tolerated but only by the good nature and acceptance of societies at large. However, 2007 heralds a change in the UK law on smoking which will no doubt see a shift in attitudes towards smokers.

Smokers have already reacted to the goodwill of non-smokers by behaving, by and large, with some respect for the right of all of us to breathe clean and smoke-free air. All of the surveys that have been conducted to date reveal that a majority of smokers would welcome a public ban on smoking as it would help to limit, or even deny, their opportunity to smoke. Thus, in effect smokers would simply have to cut down and spend less money on this very expensive habit.

As of December 2006 there have been varying degrees of legal restriction imposed on smokers depending on whereabouts in the UK you live. However, at the present time all smokers can, to some extent, smoke on the go or on the run as it were. Some can even smoke whilst they work, though this too has already been restricted to a great extent by legislation. Smokers can opt to eat and drink in places where their habit is allowed and even light up in bus shelters out of the rain.

This is all set to end within a few months. In fact, depending on when and where you bought this Simple Guide, the opportunity to smoke in public places may have already ended. If you do choose to continue to smoke after the ban on smoking in public places, you will certainly find it even more difficult to accommodate your very expensive habit. You will have to search even harder for opportunities to light up. Even before the ban is introduced, most smokers already have to excuse themselves and step outside to light up when visiting offices, shops, public buildings or the homes of non-smoking friends. This will become even more widespread and commonplace for smokers who wish to continue smoking after the full ban is implemented on 1st July 2007. The opportunities when it will be possible to attend to the habit will have to be more carefully managed and spread throughout the day. In short, smokers will have to plan their days far more carefully and be prepared to suffer the consequences of withdrawal symptoms repeatedly. Make no mistake, it's going to get a lot tougher to be a smoker.

Even if anyone questions the likely impact that the forthcoming restrictions on smoking will have on them, let us be certain about one thing at least – smoking kills. It destroys the lives of smokers and their loved ones. There is no getting away from this – hard facts about smoking are printed in simple text on all cigarette packs. It really is time to sit up and take notice as these messages are telling the truth.

Nicotine – cause and effect

NICOTINE – CAUSE AND EFFECT

Tobacco smoke is made up of more than 4,000 constituents, around 250 of which are toxic and about 60 of which can cause cancer. But it is the relatively safe component in tobacco – nicotine – that gets you hooked to smoking. It is important to understand that it is also the way that nicotine is delivered into your body in tobacco smoke that makes it so addictive. Nicotine replacement therapy (NRT) products on the other hand deliver nicotine in a variety of novel ways that mean the dose you receive is controlled so that your craving can be satisfied whilst your addiction subsides.

THE FIRST CIGARETTE OF THE DAY

As you are no doubt fully aware, nicotine is the addictive component in tobacco. In fact, nicotine is widely considered to be one of the most powerfully addictive drugs known to man. Even hardened drug addicts who come to me on a daily basis for treatment for their addictions admit that the pull of nicotine is sometimes as great (or even greater) than that of cocaine or heroin.

When you wake up after a night's sleep, levels of nicotine in your bloodstream are extremely low. The immediate signal processed by your brain is the need to replenish the level of nicotine in order to stop withdrawal symptoms from kicking in. A few minutes after waking up you will begin to physically feel the

Nicotine – cause and effect

effects of a lack of nicotine in your body. One obvious solution to this is to light up a cigarette and push back and control the withdrawal… there, that's better… or is it? There's a clear downside to that first (and subsequent) cigarette of the day. Although you've started your day by satisfying your craving for nicotine, at the same time you are also topping up on the levels of cancer-causing and toxic chemicals in your bloodstream.

Most cigarettes contain approximately 6–9 mg of nicotine within the processed tobacco, but all that's required is a few milligrams of vaporised nicotine to reach the brain for the effects to be felt. As this is the first cigarette you will have had for several hours, the effect on the lungs and brain is felt more sharply as the replenishment process accelerates the gradient of the nicotine level in your bloodstream and it rises rapidly.

The chemicals from a cigarette proceed in your blood from your lungs straight to your heart which is expecting and in need of oxygen. It certainly isn't expecting toxic substances. One

---

It's really important that you understand why smoking is so bad for you and for those around you so that you are motivated to quit.

As soon as you feel convinced that you are ready to commit yourself to quitting smoking for good, move on to *Time for action* (page 37).

of the rapid effects from smoking a cigarette is an increase in your heart rate by up to 20 beats per minute. This rapid heart rate causes your blood pressure to rise. There are lots of reasons why high blood pressure is bad. High blood pressure causes strokes, heart disease and kidney disease, but the effect you will notice with that first cigarette of the day is a feeling of dizziness and a satisfaction that you have met your craving for nicotine.

As a smoker, you may feel that you are getting a buzz out of your first cigarette of the day, particularly when there is a need to get moving and start the day's routine. But be warned – it's a false and a dangerous start to anyone's day.

SO WHAT ELSE IS GOING ON?

One of the most powerful chemicals that you're inhaling in every puff of tobacco smoke is carbon monoxide. This is highly toxic and even relatively low doses of carbon monoxide from just a few cigarettes can cause dizziness and nausea.

For more information see **Blood pressure**

Most importantly, inhaling carbon monoxide reduces your blood's ability to carry oxygen. Carbon monoxide effectively blocks the carriage of oxygen in the bloodstream, leaving your body's organs and cells starved of oxygen. To emphasise this point even further, it is well worth remembering that larger doses of carbon monoxide can prove to be fatal. Remember, the potential danger from carbon monoxide poisoning is one of the main reasons why domestic gas appliances need to be checked on a regular basis to ensure that there's no leakage of this odourless and sinister gas.

You can read more about the toxic effects of carbon monoxide in the *What happens normally?* section in *Simple extras* (page 96).

WHY DO I SEEM TO FEEL 'BETTER' AFTER I'VE LIT UP?

The spread of nicotine throughout the nervous system affects the brain and, as a consequence, our thoughts, feelings and moods. Unsurprisingly, withdrawal of nicotine from anyone for whom nicotine has become a normal stimulant often causes anxiety, stress and depression. A smoker will also often experience headaches and tiredness due to nicotine withdrawal.

As a result smokers say they feel 'stressed out' and may reach for another cigarette to try and calm themselves down. They often claim that the emergence of these symptoms is one of the main reasons why they put off trying to quit. It would seem that the only logical solution from a smoker's perspective is to continue to top up the nicotine reservoir to stop these unwanted symptoms from overtaking the body. In other words, they have to keep smoking regularly to avoid withdrawal symptoms and maintain a sense of normality.

What an incredibly powerful and addictive drug! No wonder tobacco companies have tried so hard over the years (and have been very successful) to persuade people to start smoking in the first place!

BUT SMOKING KEEPS ME THIN...

Smoking affects most of our body's functions to some extent. However, some of these effects are far more noticeable and measurable than others.

One of the main effects of the spikes of nicotine delivered in tobacco smoke is on two important glands that sit on top of our kidneys. These are called the adrenal glands and, when stimulated by nicotine, they release the hormone, adrenaline, into the bloodstream.

You will, no doubt, have heard of adrenaline. It is a natural hormone and is perhaps best known for stimulating the 'Fright, Fight, Flight' response. In essence, adrenaline helps to put us on alert enabling us to react quickly in an emergency. In prehistory when our ancestors lived in caves it was adrenaline that enabled them to run away from that sabre-toothed tiger or to fight off those aggressive Neanderthal neighbours. You may remember the last time you had a fright. The shot of adrenaline into your bloodstream from your adrenal glands would have caused your heart rate and blood pressure to rise, your breathing rate to increase and more oxygen to be diverted to your muscles. Your body was basically priming you to fight or to run away.

Another effect of adrenaline is to stimulate a rise in our blood sugar (glucose) levels, which in turn makes us less hungry than we would normally feel. So a smoking-induced release of adrenaline therefore reduces your appetite. This is why many smokers claim (sometimes in justification for continuing with their habit) that 'smoking keeps them thin'.

Nicotine – cause and effect

... AND ANYWAY, FOOD ISN'T ALL THAT IMPORTANT TO ME

Smoking dulls our sensation of taste, which is another factor in why a smoker's appetite may be suppressed. "Hang on though. Beer and crisps still taste great. And I love a curry after a drink and a smoke down the pub." But wait until you quit and then you'll see how much better your food tastes and smells.

As a smoker it's impossible to experience the full flavour of foods. As a consequence food is generally less interesting to eat. A classic response to quitting tobacco is that ex-smokers find that they have to reduce the amount of spice and salt they add to their food. Curries taste far hotter than they had previously and food in general seems to taste far more exciting and more complex. It's little wonder then that food doesn't particularly interest you at the moment. However, just try to think of the increased pleasure you'll experience in restaurants and at home when you quit. Some more food for thought then!

AM I REALLY ADDICTED... SURELY IT'S JUST A HABIT THAT I COULD BREAK AT ANYTIME?

You probably regard smoking as a good way to relax. The more stressful the situation you find yourself in, the greater your urge is to have a cigarette. So, inevitably your consumption will go up during stressful periods.

Think about the last busy, stressful day you had at work. No doubt during the day you were really looking forward to getting home or going down the pub and having a drink to go with a cigarette or two (or even three!). That way you get a double dose of relaxing chemicals! There is also a sharing experience associated with smoking and drinking which is why people often smoke in the company of other smokers. "You smoke too? Great! Let's have a drink and a fag together!" But soon all of us will be able to enjoy a drink or two with our family and friends in the clean smoke-free atmosphere of our local pub. In fact, if you live in Scotland or Ireland you are even luckier, and can already enjoy smoke-free public places.

All drugs of addiction share a common theme – they are habit-forming and are best shared with others. Smoking is frequently associated with other drug use, and in particular alcohol (another drug which can be abused through addiction).

However, our bodies deal with alcohol in a very different way to how they deal with nicotine. Our bodies have evolved a very powerful mechanism to remove alcohol, providing we don't overpower this mechanism

by overdoing it. Two or three drinks two or three times a week will be okay for most of us. However, any more than this, particularly lots of alcohol in one session (binge drinking), is not so good! This mechanism involves a natural enzyme called alcohol dehydrogenase which detoxifies and removes alcohol from our systems with reasonable speed and efficiency. It is alcohol dehydrogenase that enables us to enjoy an occasional beer or glass of wine without any serious ill effects, providing we moderate our consumption. With tobacco we are not so lucky though. The toxic chemicals inhaled in tobacco smoke are very difficult for the body to recognise and handle, even when consumed in small quantities. Remember though that nicotine is the highly addictive but relatively safe constituent in tobacco smoke. It's the other stuff that we expose ourselves and others to that causes cancers, heart attacks and strokes.

One is the loneliest number!

Think about how you feel when you are the only one lighting up? Or when you have to go outside to have a fag whilst all your friends are having a social drink and a laugh together? And yes, admit it. Although you may not notice the smell yourself, you probably notice how some of your friends turn their noses up when you return smelling, even stinking of 'l'air du fag'.

Virtually all smokers agree with the fact that having to smoke alone – either to go outside or removing themselves from a smoke-free area – tends to remove the enjoyment from those cigarettes. You just need it, and sometimes crave it, to stave off the inevitable consequences of not smoking.

So, the answer to the question at the beginning of this section is… yes – you are addicted!

Being addicted is something that we can and will deal with in this guide. The real problem with tobacco is that it is the only legal product available on common sale which can kill you even when used in apparently small quantities. So by all means start by cutting down but don't get stuck on a few fags a day! Don't despair! Read on, you are well on your way to understanding why your aim must be to quit smoking for good!

> If you feel like you've read enough and are now ready to commit yourself to quitting smoking for good, please move on to *Time for action* (page 37).

WHAT ABOUT THE FINANCIAL ASPECTS OF SMOKING?

A common issue that is often raised regarding smoking is the issue of the financial costs associated with the habit, not only for the individual smoker but also for society as a whole.

Many people assume that without duty from the sale of tobacco, as taxpayers we would all end up paying more in income tax and VAT to make up the shortfall. Indeed, the arguments continue to circulate about the tax issue and smoking bans, and the situation is certainly complex.

One positive aspect of quitting smoking, and one of the most commonly cited reasons that so many people take a decision to quit, is the fact you will have far more money in your pocket to spend on far better and healthier things. Why not take a look at the box below

Assuming you previously smoked 20 cigarettes a day and a pack of 20 cigarettes now costs about a fiver, you could be saving:

- £35.00 per week, enough for a nice meal out.
- £150 per month, enough for a weekend trip away.
- £1,825 per year, enough to take that exotic holiday you've always dreamed about.
- £18,250 over a decade, you could begin to make a real dent in your mortgage.

and see what you could be saving from quitting the weed. You could even think about using some of your extra wealth to treat yourself to an incentive to make sure you keep yourself smoke-free.

But if every smoker were to quit and tobacco taxes dried up, where would the Government get the lost revenue from? Well, as a direct result of the new-found individual wealth in the hands of ex-smokers, public spending on all goods and services would rise in line with the amount that would have previously been spent on tobacco. The Government would therefore recover money through increased VAT, increased income tax through increased employment and more corporation tax from more profitable companies. One method of estimating the cost of smoking is to apply the criteria used to estimate the value of the loss of a human life. The Department of Transport, for example, put this value at £680,590 in 1997. If this value is applied to the total number of deaths attributable to smoking, the cost of smoking-related mortality in the UK at 1997 prices is just under £80 billion (source: Action on Smoking and Health [ASH]).

In addition, we shouldn't neglect the very positive effect on the NHS of quitting smoking. In 1998, the NHS spend on treating smoking-related disease was estimated at a massive £1.7 billion (yes that's right, one thousand seven hundred million pounds in only one year).

I think that we can all safely assume that the Government has done its sums and calculated that any loss in taxes raised from tobacco would be more than made up for by savings and additional spending elsewhere. At least, no politician is having any second thoughts about the smoking ban and it is being widely accepted by both smokers and non-smokers to be a positive thing for the UK.

So don't worry about the amount of tax you won't be paying when you quit smoking for good! The Government will manage, and you can spend what you save on something else like a holiday or something for your grandchildren who you have a much better chance of seeing grow up. And why sacrifice your health just to keep the Chancellor's coffers full?

Nicotine – cause and effect

Risks versus benefits

RISKS VERSUS BENEFITS

If you smoke, ask yourself this question – why do I wear a seat belt in a car? To phrase it differently, if you smoke whilst you drive, you may wish to ask yourself what purpose your seat belt is serving.

Everyone takes risks in life. Some are simply unavoidable. For example, we all take journeys in planes, trains and automobiles and all of us will cross busy roads on a daily basis. Some slightly more risky activities are the preserve of the thrill seeker. Some people jump out of a perfectly serviceable aircraft with nothing more than a strong sheet of silk and polyester strapped to their backs (that's a parachute to you and me). Others climb high mountains, go abseiling, ride motorbikes and even hang-glide.

None of these activities though compares to the mortal risk that you are exposing yourself to by smoking cigarettes. It is a fact that up to half of all long-term smokers will die prematurely from smoking-related diseases. In addition, virtually all smokers will be exposing their bodies to serious long-term damage and will be risking a lifetime of ill health.

To put the relative risks of smoking and other risk-taking behaviour into some context, each year about 5,000 people are killed or seriously injured in motor-related accidents in the UK. This compares with approximately

120,000 people who die prematurely from smoking-related diseases each year. To put this into even more perspective:

- 5,000 is the average crowd at a league 2 football match.
- 120,000 is the approximate population of the city of Oxford.

Perhaps even more illuminating is the observation that the tragedy of 9/11 at the World Trade Centre in New York City claimed the lives of the equivalent UK death toll from just 1 week of smoking.

If you still feel you need more convincing of the relative risk of smoking compared with other risk-taking activities why not ask an insurance broker and examine the forms that have to be filled out for life insurance. Insurance companies have a wealth of statistics at their disposal regarding the relative risks of various activities and lifestyles. Remember, they are in the business of ensuring that their risk (not yours) of having to pay out on a policy is covered by the premium that you pay.

So let's think about removing one dangerous, extremely risky but completely avoidable activity from your life, one where the roulette wheel spins and the odds are stacked against you – smoking.

Of course all of us will die eventually, like taxes, death is certain. However, all of us want to live long, productive and healthy lives. Or most of us do anyway. It is perfectly normal for humans to want to gain the best length and quality of life whilst on this earth. All of us will enjoy moments in our lives which keep us going through the bad times.

However, smoking denies many people the opportunity for a long and healthy life. Smoking is a major cause of heart attacks and strokes and has been proven to cause many cancers, including lung, mouth and stomach cancer to name just three. In fact, the list of smoking-related cancers makes for truly scary reading. I probably don't need to tell you that there are better ways to die.

So reduce your risk of dying from a smoking-induced heart attack or cancer and make a commitment to quit smoking for good today! If you do quit, you will also be reducing your risk of a whole array of other long-proven smoking-induced illnesses together with the following more recently discovered consequences of smoking:

- impotence
- premature death of your baby (or cot death)
- blindness.

If you smoke, it is almost guaranteed that you will die before your time. Nobody wants to die before their natural time is up. Going back to the analogy at the start of the section, that's why nearly all of us wear a seat belt during car journeys. We know only too well the consequences of not belting up if we were to be involved in a road accident. If we apply this simple safety rule to all our behaviour, we would reduce all unnecessary risks in life. It therefore follows and logic dictates that we shouldn't smoke.

WHAT IS DANGEROUS IN CIGARETTE SMOKE?

Smoke from tobacco doesn't only act as a transporter of nicotine. As I mentioned earlier, nicotine is the relatively safe component of tobacco compared with a cocktail of other chemicals that make up cigarette smoke. Up to 4,000 substances, 60 of which are known to be carcinogenic (cancer producing) and 250 known to be toxic are lurking within that cloud of grey wispy smoke.

Here are a few of the more common chemicals found in tobacco smoke. Some of them are real tongue twisters and all are highly dangerous:

- carbon monoxide
- benzaldehyde
- butyric acid
- decanoic acid
- hexanoic acid
- 3-methylbutyraldehyde.

The link between smoking and lung cancer was first discovered in the early 1950s. Despite some early resistance and denial from the large tobacco corporations, even they have eventually conceded that smoking is a highly dangerous habit that causes cancer, and not just lung cancer but many other forms such as throat, bladder, stomach and lip cancer.

NOT EVERYONE WHO SMOKES GETS CANCER SO WHAT OTHER DISEASES COULD I GET?

Even if you are lucky enough to escape cancer, as a smoker the chances are that as you grow older your lung capacity will begin to diminish. You'll probably begin to find that taking the stairs or running for the bus is becoming increasingly arduous as your breathing becomes more and more restricted and difficult. As a smoker, your lungs are not able to process enough oxygen into the bloodstream due to a reduction in their capacity to extract oxygen from the atmosphere.

Many people who smoke go on to develop a condition called Chronic Obstructive Pulmonary Disease (COPD). People with severe cases of COPD often end up relying on oxygen from a cylinder as well as needing a whole range of medicines to help them breathe.

As well as this, smokers are also more prone to infections of the respiratory system such as bronchitis and pneumonia as well as practically any other infectious respiratory disease. It's not a pretty sight! Even if your doctor prescribes you antibiotics, chances are that they won't work as well as they would for a non-smoker. One of the most depressing aspects of being a practising healthcare professional is to witness and monitor the slow but sure decline in a smoker's health.

You can read more about how smoking affects the lungs and circulation in the *What happens normally?* section in *Simple extras* (page 96).

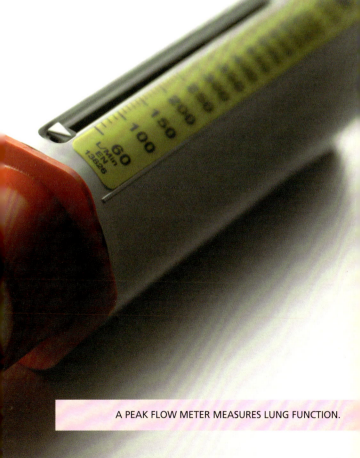

A PEAK FLOW METER MEASURES LUNG FUNCTION.

I'M NEARLY CONVINCED, BUT MY GRANDDAD LIVED TILL HE WAS 85 AND SMOKED ALL HIS LIFE. SO WHY CAN'T I?

Those who smoked and lived to a ripe old age were the lucky few. Ask around a bit! Where are these ancient smokers? Take a look in your local cemetery at some of the headstones and calculate how many people died in their 40s, 50s and 60s in the last 30 years. Far too many!

A lucky few do manage to slip through the net and escape the deadly onslaught of 4,000 chemicals contained within cigarette smoke. It is thought that this lucky minority of smokers may have some sort of protective gene which guards against cancer growth.

But don't play Russian roulette with your life! Your chances of surviving into old age and collecting your pension are not good if you continue to smoke. Remember the facts about the likely causes of death in the UK. Smoking is the number one preventable cause of death by a long way – even if you do hang-glide every weekend.

Convinced yet? If so and you are ready to commit yourself to quitting smoking for good move on to *Time for action* (page 37).

I'VE HEARD SMOKING CAN AFFECT YOUR SKIN AND THE WAY YOU LOOK – IS THIS RIGHT?

You're right. The effect that smoking has on skin is fairly awful. Look through any celebrity magazine, and spot those who are over 40, and see if you can tell the smokers from the non-smokers. It becomes easy after a while and if you're an expert celebrity watcher, you can even begin to tell the ones who used to smoke but have now quit.

A popular Channel 4 'reality' TV programme recently looked at how people could make themselves look 10 years younger. All the contestants chosen by the producers were men or women who were smokers. After all, if you're going to pick a person who looks older than they ought to, just pick a smoker. It's an obvious choice! All of the people chosen for the programmes were instructed to quit smoking as part of their make-over as there seemed little point in working against the toxic tide of cigarette smoke.

Another unwelcome side-effect of smoking has recently been publicised by the Government – impotence in men (or erectile dysfunction as the experts call it). As mentioned earlier, it really does seem that fags drain away your manhood!

From the moment any smoker quits the habit, their skin tone, colour and texture will start to improve and eventually will return to normal. Nature has a much more lasting effect than any make-up or cosmetic surgery. Start smoking again and your skin will rapidly deteriorate. Many young people who quit smoking cite vanity as a major trigger along with money considerations and being involved with a partner who is a non-smoker.

And please, you might not notice it but you need to know that non-smokers (you know those attractive people with healthy complexions), always notice the awful stink that smoke brings in its wake – your clothes, your hair, your skin and most noticeably – your breath. Sorry to keep pointing this out but sometimes even the best of friends find it hard to impart facts like these!

Risks versus benefits

SO YOU'RE SAYING THAT EVERYTHING ABOUT ME WILL IMPROVE?

If you quit smoking for good, it shouldn't take too long before you notice that you start to feel and look a whole lot better. Okay, immediately after you quit you may notice that you are coughing up a bit more phlegm than you would otherwise do and you may also notice that you get a few more colds and bugs. But remember – these are short-term sacrifices for a whole host of long-term benefits.

Eventually you will notice that your skin complexion returns to normal and starts to look fresher and clearer. Your breathing will become easier and you will notice that run for the bus or the dash upstairs is not the problem it used to be. Other parts of your body also begin to start to function normally again. Your taste buds will experience a revival and that awful stale smell of tobacco will evaporates from your hair, skin, clothes and, most importantly, your breath.

WHAT ABOUT PASSIVE SMOKING?

Yes, passive smoking is a real issue. It has been estimated that anyone who smokes 20 cigarettes a day in and around their home will be forcing the equivalent of 180 cigarettes each year on anyone else who lives in that house. That means your kids and your pets are getting toxic doses whether you like it or not. Even if you smoke outside the house, measurements inside reveal levels of smoke particles higher than in non-smoking households.

The only people that won't commit or admit to the passive smoking issue are those that work for the tobacco cartels. We all know it is dangerous at every level and this is the reason why the Government is banning smoking from all public places in 2007.

The sooner the better, for all concerned!

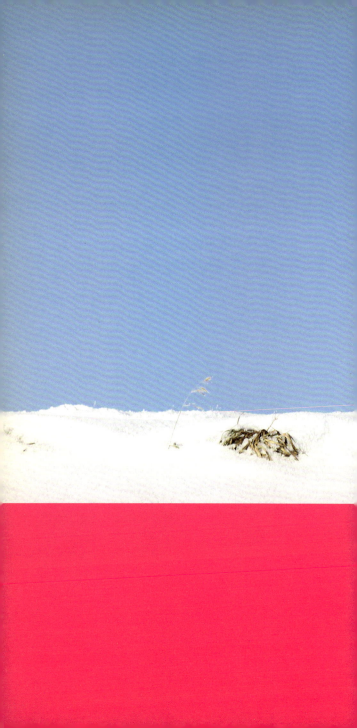

Time for action

TIME FOR ACTION

For any smoker to quit smoking, a series of positive steps need to be taken. Action is needed and now is the time!

DUMP THE DENIAL!

One of the main conditions necessary for a smoker to continue smoking is an absolute attachment to denial. All smokers and other substance addicts engage in denial. Without denial, a smoker cannot continue. So, denial is the first hurdle to overcome.

Admit that you're addicted and cannot control your habit. In fact, it controls you. Tobacco controls your behaviour, your movements and your attitudes. Without removing and squashing your withdrawal symptoms, you cannot think straight.

Once you accept this fact, its time to take back control of your life. When you, rather than tobacco, have control you can stop looking for times (you need 6 minutes on average to smoke a cigarette) and places to smoke. You can relax a bit more, you don't need time out to remove that craving and, more importantly, you have

Drop the denial, dump it and you have passed the first qualifying round.

> Beat the denial. Admit it, you WANT to stop, you NEED to stop and you are GOING to stop.

overcome your reckless behaviour! Punch the air – you can win and overcome it. You're going to take charge. You **can** overcome your need for the weed!

Remember ALL smoking careers have to end one way or another

Most smokers find that they come to a point in their life when their habit has to stop. This can be for a wide variety of reasons. Most, however, are based on love, money, guilt and health.

The smoker is usually compelled into action by a combination of common personal triggers such as:

- ill health
- moving house
- the arrival of a new baby
- extra financial commitments
- being prevented at work and play from smoking.

All of these triggers contribute to the reasons for quitting smoking. Two outcomes of stopping are certain as with life, death and taxes mentioned earlier. You will pay less TAX, and therefore have more disposable income in your pocket, and you will postpone your natural DEATH.

GET HELP!

A wealth of evidence clearly shows that your best chance of quitting smoking for good comes from a combination of professional support together with proven treatments including nicotine replacement therapy and other prescription drugs.

There are a whole host of people who claim that they can help you to quit smoking. You only have to look in your local newspapers and yellow pages to find the details of acupuncturists, hypnotists, herbalists and a whole variety of other pay-as-you-go possibilities. However, before you respond to these offers of help, please remember that the only scientifically proven methods for successful quitting involve nicotine replacement therapy and some drugs that are available on prescription, particularly when these products are used in combination with professional support. These interventions are discussed in detail in *Stop smoking products* (page 59).

Although you may see advertisements for all kinds of weird and wonderful cures for smoking it is important that you realise that there is very little published data (and in many cases none at all) that will support their claims. If you have any doubts about any remedy that you are offered, ask to see the published evidence that backs up their claims. I have met far too many smokers in the past who have parted with large sums of money for 'snake-oil' remedies only to relapse or fail later down the line.

MAKE THE CALL – IT'S FREE!

One of the many things that the NHS does well is to help smokers quit the habit. This help involves a variety of evidence-based interventions that have been scientifically proven to work. All you have to do is ring the national helpline (0800 169 0169) and you will be given a number for your local service who will then direct you to a trained stop smoking adviser. There is also a great NHS website at *www.gosmokefree.co.uk* that essentially has the same role as the free phone number.

There are many other great sources of help available to the quitter. One example is Quit (*www.quit.org.uk*), which is run by an independent charity whose mission is to save lives by helping smokers to stop. This service provides a free confidential advice line (Quitline) on 0800 00 22 00, which is manned by a team of professionally trained quit smoking advisers. They also offer an email counselling service (*stopsmoking@quit.org.uk*).

The Government is backing up the forthcoming public smoking ban with funding for stop smoking services on the NHS. It is finally using its authority to push and pull! Although they are telling you that you really ought to stop, they are making it known that help is available when you decide that smoking is no longer for you. In other words, the Government is essentially telling you that now is the time to quit!

The maths are simple. The Government reckons that at least £1.7 billion is spent on treatment each year and for every smoker who quits for good, we can expect to save £80,000 in healthcare costs. The best medicine is preventative medicine. This is public health in its simplest form.

PROFESSIONAL SUPPORT

NHS stop smoking advisers are mainly drawn from four groups:

- specialist advisers
- pharmacists
- practice nurses
- GPs.

Probably the best approach for smokers who are about to embark on a quit smoking journey is to locate a specialist stop smoking adviser through their local stop smoking service. As described in the last section, your local service can be located by ringing the national helpline (0800 169 0169) or alternatively through NHS direct on 0845 46 47 – just give them your postcode and they will do the rest!

Pharmacist advisers are almost exclusively based in accessible local pharmacies and these professionals are often the easiest for most people to approach and access. Alternatively you could call into your local surgery and make an appointment to see a practice nurse or a GP, or you can enquire if there is a specialist stop smoking counsellor available within the surgery (which is becoming increasingly commonplace). Remember, you are free to approach whichever healthcare professional you prefer to see in whatever environment suits you best. Just remember to make sure that you check with whomever you chose to ensure that they are appropriately trained to offer stop smoking advice. Do not assume that your GP, practice nurse or pharmacist has specialist stop smoking training, as most do not. If they do not, ask them to point you in the direction of a professional who has.

You should always bear in mind that specialist quit smoking advisers have acquired their knowledge and expertise in stopping smoking not only through training but also through many years of experience from working directly with people who want to quit smoking. Many, like myself, have had years of experience in dealing with tobacco addiction and can therefore relate closely to the problems and difficulties that you will face when trying to quit cigarettes.

It is probable that your local stop smoking service will direct you to the most convenient and accessible service provider close to your home or office. You should grab this offer with both hands and take the plunge. Nothing ventured, nothing gained, even if the person you are going to enrol with is unknown to you. Any kind of help is better than no help whatsoever. You should also remember that the NHS isn't the only one saving money – you will be too.

YOU'RE ON YOUR WAY... NOW STICK WITH IT!

Once you have contacted your local stop smoking service, you may be invited to attend a number of one-to-one sessions with your stop smoking adviser or alternatively you may be offered group counselling.

One-to-one sessions are usually conducted on a weekly basis and you may be invited to attend at least four sessions. Look forward to these meetings and try as much as possible to ensure that you can attend and do turn up. Showing your face at such encounters will be part of the motivational drive that keeps you on track to a smoke-free existence. However,

Time for action

if you find it difficult to attend these regular one-to-one appointments, more and more stop smoking services are now offering telephone support services, which can be a useful alternative.

During your encounters with specialist quit smoking services, it will be usual for a counsellor to use a carbon monoxide detector at each visit. Feel free to ask for a test at any time – it will show you just how much pure air your lungs are getting and how quickly you can rid yourself of this poisonous gas. A high reading (11 parts per million or more) will

indicate that your lungs are expelling carbon monoxide from recently smoked cigarettes. A reading under 5 parts per million would normally indicate that you are smoke free and effectively a non-smoker!

If you book into a pharmacy quit smoking service, the pharmacist will ask you to attend sessions which will be linked to the supply of 7 days of nicotine replacement therapy. One advantage of this approach is that the adviser can also supply drug therapy at the same time.

If you choose to go to a GP's surgery for stop smoking advice you will probably either see the practice nurse or, as is becoming increasingly commonplace, another member of staff who has received appropriate training and who can offer you additional support. However, it is important to be aware that very few GPs in the UK will be able to offer you counselling directly. Your GP though may be able to provide you with a prescription for all forms of nicotine replacement therapy and other drugs such as Zyban® or Champix® (see *Stop smoking products,* page 59). However, it is important to remember that if you choose to use these products you should also seek support from an appropriately trained adviser as this will greatly increase your chances of quitting for good!

Some Primary Care Organisations (PCOs) fund and extend one-to-one sessions with stop smoking advisers beyond the four sessions described previously. However, you should check to see what the standard practice in your area is. Most PCTs will also offer group counselling sessions which can also be very helpful. Walk-in centres also offer varying types of contact with trained advisers with some even offering evening and weekend appointments which may suit those who find normal working hours prevent them from attending sessions or appointments.

REACHING FOR THE NEW YOU!

You will certainly face many hurdles along your journey to quit smoking for good. Probably the main obstacle you will face will be the old you and your old ways and habits. That quick drink in the pub after work or a night out with mates in the wine bar all add up to smoking encounters that you need to think of as a thing of the past. You should consider your first smoke-free day as the first day of the rest of your life. This will make it easier for you to accept that your old habits and behaviour will need to change so that you can adjust to being the 'new' you.

You should avoid previous locations which reinforce your past behaviour. Go somewhere different for your after-work pint or find other ways to relax. It should certainly become a whole lot easier from the 1st July 2007 as all pubs and restaurants will be smoke-free zones across the whole of the UK.

Join a gym, go for a bike ride or simply walk more than you did as a smoker. Indeed, becoming more active is one of the fundamental changes to your lifestyle that you will find yourself making. You will, after all, have more energy as the effects of all those toxic chemicals part company with your body. The gradual departure of the toxic products from smoking will ensure that you start to feel more alive and want to become more physically active. Indeed, it has been shown that physical exercise during a quit attempt actually increases the chances of a successful quit.

POSITIVE ACTION POINTS

Make sure that you tell everyone what you are doing – that you're quitting smoking for good. This is an extremely sound tactic, as you are far less likely to relapse if everyone you know is aware that you are now a non-smoker. Tell yourself too… repeatedly! I have even known people who have put a notice in their local newspaper! You are now well on the way to divorcing yourself from the deadly weed.

No divorce is ever easy and it is often painful, but you can make it easier. It is vitally important to remove all traces of tobacco and any tobacco-related accessories from your immediate environment and, for that matter, from your life. If you put those last few fags in a drawer or hang onto your favourite lighter you are far more likely to return to being the old you. So, out must go:

- all tobacco products
- ashtrays
- lighters and matches
- visits to tobacconists
- acceptance that smoking is somehow normal
- mixing with 'dealers' (i.e. people and places who sell or offer cigarettes to you).

Like any divorce, these changes must be handled seriously and sensitively. But if you cannot access cigarettes, you won't be able to smoke even if you experience an intense craving. It's the golden rule of quitting – **don't go near any source of tobacco!**

DON'T MAKE EXCUSES

Many people who want to quit smoking worry that they will put on weight after giving up. This worry is certainly not without foundation. On average, ex-smokers appear to gain about 6–8 lbs after ditching their habit. However, it is important to remember that weight gain isn't a problem for everyone. Many people manage not to put on any weight at all as they begin to spend more of their non-smoking time doing more energetic things. However, even if you do

gain a few pounds, you can rest assured that losing that extra weight will usually be a whole lot easier than quitting smoking. And remember, even health experts agree that a slight gain in weight is certainly less dangerous than persisting with your smoking habit.

KEEP BUSY

You should also try and find new ways of occupying yourself during times that you would normally light up. For example, many people find it difficult to avoid the after dinner cigarette and this is often the first tough test that the new quitter will face. Finding a way to counter the urge to smoke after a meal is essential and you should prepare yourself accordingly. One obvious way to tackle this situation is to always eat with non-smokers – these people will not carry tobacco and therefore cannot act as your dealer and, more importantly, they won't smoke after food.

CLEAN AWAY THOSE AWFUL SMELLS

The smell of stale tobacco is repulsive and its removal is not only an essential part of the cleaning ritual, it will also transfer you to a different place – away from the old you! With your newly released income, why not treat your clothes to a visit to the dry cleaners. Take down your curtains and take them along to the cleaners too. You should also try to remove all traces of tobacco from your wardrobe and other soft furnishings. Your friends and family will instantly notice the difference in your environment and so will you.

PERSUADE SOMEONE TO QUIT WITH YOU

Many people find that quitting with a partner or a good friend can be a great way to stop smoking for good. There is one massive advantage and one big disadvantage with such an approach.

Bonding together with a loved one or good friend in a joint attempt can be a wonderful experience. You'll help, encourage and support each other, and it can also be an added bonus if you attend the same counselling sessions. Neither of you will want to be the first to succumb or fail, and so the joint effort can be a real spur to success.

The downside of this approach is that if one of you fails, the chances are so will the other. Evidence shows us that if one quitter relapses and their attempt to stop fails, the other will often quickly follow suit.

So by all means ask a friend but don't let your attempt be diverted by the behaviour of others around you. It's your life, your body and your addiction and only you can finally beat it.

DO YOUR SUMS!

Never forget just how much you have spent supporting your smoking habit. The sums are even more eye-watering the longer you smoke. For example, an average smoker on 20 a day will burn about £2,000 each year from their (already taxed) income. By giving up, you'll effectively be giving yourself a substantial pay rise – about £50 a week before tax for the average working smoker. Any way that you cut this, it amounts to a huge amount of money that you are quite literally setting fire to. Just think about what you could be doing with all that extra money you save by quitting. You could be treating yourself and your family to a nice holiday or perhaps you could be putting down a deposit on that new car you've always wanted.

Stop smoking products

STOP SMOKING PRODUCTS

You've met your adviser, so now let's look at what products and treatments there are that can help you quit. What works and what is available to add to your willpower, motivation and commitment?

WHAT'S AVAILABLE?

The short answer is… loads of stuff! Let's have a look at all the products available on the market.

NICOTINE REPLACEMENT THERAPY

We'll start with nicotine replacement therapy or NRT for short.

NRT is by far the most widely accepted and proven method of helping people quit. There are literally thousands of pages of well-conducted scientific trials that have demonstrated the effectiveness of NRT in stopping smoking. That said, like most things in life, NRT is not 100% effective, and a substantial number of people do relapse with this approach. However, this should not necessarily be taken as a failure of the NRT itself. People relapse for a whole variety of reasons and any counsellor will tell you that NRT on its own is not usually enough. This is why it is so important to seek the advice and support of a specially trained stop smoking adviser.

Stop smoking products

You should remember that NRT will not normally deliver your brain the same amount of nicotine you get from smoking a cigarette. You will not feel the same 'hit' that is produced by vaporised nicotine inhaled in cigarette smoke. This point highlights why it is so important that you remain fully motivated and determined to quit before embarking on a quit regime. NRT will do its job providing you add your own intent and willpower and also get regular support from a trained counsellor or adviser. Together, it works and the evidence shows that people do quit in substantial numbers.

There is a vast array of different NRT products available on the market and people often ask me what is the most effective option available. The answer to this is simple. No single NRT product is more effective than another. What works best for someone else may not work so well for you. At the end of the day, your choice of NRT product should be guided by what suits you and your lifestyle the most.

In the following sections, I will set out the range of NRT products that are available. Remember, all of these different NRT products are available on prescription as well as over the counter, and all work better when combined with a programme of support and advice given by a professional with expertise in stopping smoking. If you don't have to pay for your prescriptions, it is worth going to see your GP to ask for a prescription – this in effect makes your treatment free! NRT should be used for 8–10 weeks after a quit date has been set.

Nicotine patches

The skin patch is currently the most popular choice of nicotine replacement and there are three main branded products available:

- Nicorette (Pfizer)
- Nicotinell (Novartis)
- Niquitin CQ (GlaxoSmithKline)

Nicorette provides 16 hours of nicotine delivery whilst Nicotinell and Niquitin CQ are both 24-hour patches. One patch of any of these brands will last for 1 day and they are normally sold in packs of seven, which last for 1 week. Your GP or pharmacist will be able to give you an initial prescription of at least

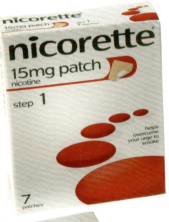

1 week's supply and then, depending on how you get on, he or she will be able to extend the supply for another 3 weeks. There may be circumstances when this treatment period can be extended even further.

Patches work by transferring a steady flow of very small amounts of nicotine through the skin and into the bloodstream. This is technically called transdermal therapy, which literally means the movement of a drug across the skin membrane into the blood vessels just below the surface. Transdermal therapy is also widely used to deliver many other drugs (for

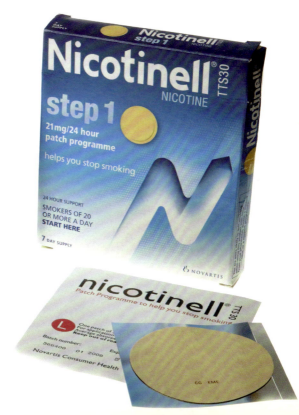

example, drugs that control sickness and pain) into our bodies. It is a very convenient form of drug delivery in that it is very discreet (no one need know that you are using a patch) and as it delivers a steady flow of nicotine it means that you don't have to remember to take additional doses or nicotine top-ups by any other means.

There are a few disadvantages with nicotine patches that you should be aware of. However, most of these can often be avoided if problems do arise. Firstly, the patch can give rise to a skin reaction and may cause an irritating rash. This problem can be lessened by switching the site of the patch each time it is applied. For most people, however, the rash subsides pretty quickly. The second problem is that the 24-hour patches can give rise to strange dreams and sleep disturbances. If this is troublesome for you, then simply remove the patch at night or instead switch to the 16-hour patch.

Each type of patch is available in three different strengths. The 16-hour patches contain 15 mg, 10 mg or 5 mg of nicotine whilst the 24-hour patches contain 21 mg, 14 mg or 7 mg. In essence, these different patches provide you with a structured approach to the management of your withdrawal symptoms and cravings that you can adjust to suit your individual needs. However, contrary to popular belief, the available evidence does not appear to warrant a step down approach in which the dose of nicotine patch is gradually reduced over time in an effort to wean you off nicotine replacement therapy. In fact, the evidence shows that it is as

Stop smoking products

least as effective to remain on the most appropriate dose for you for your entire quit attempt and then to simply stop using the NRT patches at the appropriate time as directed by your quit smoking adviser.

Quit smoking for good!

Nicotine gum

Nicotine chewing gum is very popular with those who feel that they can control their habit simply by chewing a piece of gum as and when their craving kicks in. Nicotine gum is available in two strengths – 2 and 4 mg – and is provided under the same brand names by the same three companies that manufacture the patches described in the last section.

The amount of nicotine gum you need to use is very much dependent on your strength

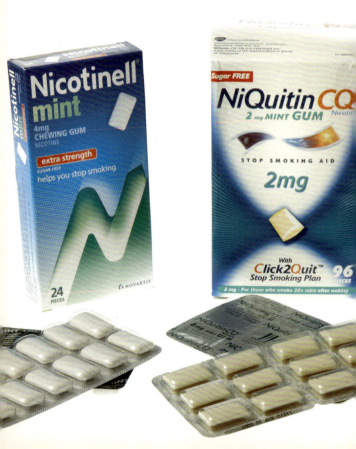

of craving. Manufacturers normally recommend that you can chew no more than a maximum of 15 pieces a day, but the amount you chew can be varied to suit your individual needs and cravings. The stronger 4 mg dose of gum should be used if you are just embarking on your quit programme and you have normally smoked **more** than 20 cigarettes a day. The lower 2 mg strength should be used if you are either starting to reduce your usage of nicotine gum or if you have smoked fewer than 20 cigarettes a day prior to quitting.

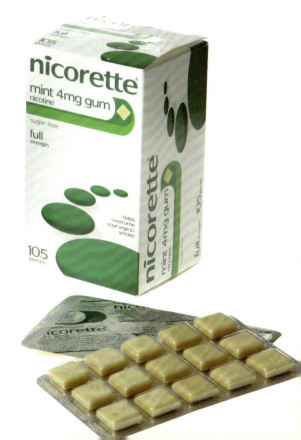

There are a number of problems that may arise from nicotine gum, most of which occur as a consequence of how the gum is chewed. To overcome these problems, you will need to adopt a slightly different method of chewing NRT gum compared with how you would use normal chewing gum. The proper way to use NRT gum is to chew a piece slowly until the flavour starts to fade. The gum should then be left to rest between your gum and your cheek so that absorption of nicotine can continue through the lining of the mouth and into your blood stream. Once the flavour has gone, the gum can then be chewed once more and then re-parked against your mouth lining to extract the last remaining nicotine content.

Nicotine, when chewed in the form of gum, can cause a burning sensation in the mouth and users often find that it is impossible to chew 15 pieces a day due to this effect. However, it is always possible to break a piece in half and reduce the amount chewed if that helps to prevent reaching for a fag and the dreaded relapse.

Another disadvantage with nicotine gum relates to a behavioural issue. As nicotine levels from chewing nicotine gum rise and fall more or less in line with smoking cigarettes, you may feel a desire to smoke between each piece of gum you use. In contrast, a nicotine patch will maintain a constant level of nicotine in the blood and should therefore dissuade you from smoking whilst the patch is applied. Consequently, you will probably need to have a little more self-discipline if you choose to use nicotine gum to help you quit.

The Nicorette brand of gum and the inhalator (see page 74) have now been issued with a licence for reducing smoking. This means that smokers who don't want to completely quit smoking outright can use these products in an effort to reduce the amount of cigarettes smoked day by day. The principle underpinning this approach is that the smoker will cut down over a period of a few months to a level of smoking at which they feel able to attempt a full quit. The gum or inhalator can then be phased out slowly so that NRT is eventually stopped. The manufacturers of Nicorette call this 'Cut Down Then Stop' or CDTS for short. It is important to remember that the best kind of quit attempt for most smokers is an outright supported quit attempt and that CDTS should only be for the relatively few smokers who would otherwise not consider stopping at all.

Quit smoking for good!

Nicotine lozenges

Nicotine lozenges are made by two companies – Novartis and GlaxoSmithKline. They are recommended for use in much the same way as nicotine chewing gum – replacing cigarettes with an oral form of nicotine – and the guidance given for nicotine gum also applies to this form of NRT.

Some people report that nicotine lozenges do not appear to cause the same amount of burning as nicotine gum, but these reports vary widely according to individual experiences. Although lozenges do not appear to be as popular as gum forms of NRT, there is currently no evidence to suggest that they are not equally effective as gum in dealing with nicotine withdrawal symptoms.

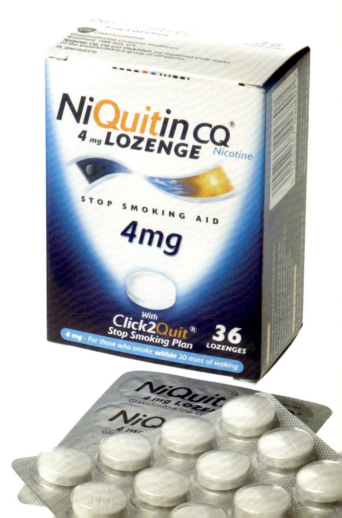

Nicotine nasal spray

There is currently only one branded nicotine nasal spray available on the market (Nicorette). However, this form of NRT can be a very useful method for assisting with quit programmes. The NRT spray offers the smoker a real 'hit' of nicotine and is the closest treatment option to a real cigarette in terms of the speed and potency of nicotine action. It certainly delivers a higher and faster dose of nicotine than any of the other NRT options including the patch, gum or lozenge.

So why isn't the nasal spray the number one choice for NRT? The simplest reason is that its use is often accompanied by substantial pain and discomfort; when used as directed it can sting the inside of the nose and the back of the throat and can cause watering of the eyes. This discomfort can last for up to several minutes, although these symptoms usually become less severe after a week or so of use. However, for those who feel that this NRT approach appeals to them and can cope with these side-effects and adjust to the method of delivery, then it can be a real winner.

The nasal spray is particularly useful for a smoker who has developed a 30 a day plus habit.

Stop smoking products

The inhalator

The inhalator is a device designed to address the habit of holding a cigarette. It looks like a simple cigarette holder – a white plastic tube with a tapered end for clenching in the mouth. The device has a designated space inside for loading a nicotine soaked plug or cartridge. Once this is activated by closing and locking the two halves together, the nicotine can be released by inhaling or sucking on the holder. It therefore mimics a real cigarette holder but without the cigarette!

The nicotine that is released permeates through the lining of the mouth but not into the lungs. This means that the levels of nicotine in the blood will be low, but will still be high enough to hold back the craving sensation and any withdrawal symptoms. By providing a source of nicotine in this way and also satisfying the hand-to-mouth action associated with smoking a normal cigarette, many smokers find that this method can be very helpful in their quest to quit. However, others would argue that dumping the hand-to-mouth habit is critical for their personal success and therefore reject the idea of the inhalator. Nevertheless, I would always advise keeping an open mind on all versions of NRT before settling on which method works best for you.

Stop smoking products

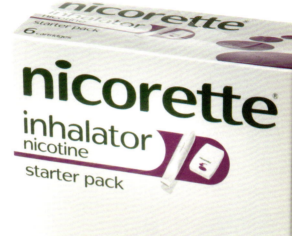

Nicotine microtabs

The microtab is the latest NRT option that has been made available on the market. These small tablets contain 2 mg of nicotine and should be placed under the tongue so that they slowly disperse. They should not be swallowed or chewed. As a result the nicotine is slowly released and, like the inhalator, lozenge or gum, levels of nicotine in the bloodstream slowly rise to suppress the craving. The main advantage of using nicotine microtabs is that they are very discreet. They can therefore be used in circumstances where you might find yourself wanting to smoke but have no means of secretly suppressing the craving. Like any other NRT product, your personal circumstances will dictate whether or not this is the best option available to you.

A SUMMARY OF NRT PRODUCTS AVAILABLE

NRT product	Low strength	Medium strength	High strength
Patches (16 hour)	5 mg	10 mg	15 mg
Patches (24 hour)	7 mg	14 mg	21 mg
Gum	2 mg	–	4 mg
Lozenges	1 mg/2 mg	–	4 mg
Nasal spray	–	–	0.5 mg
Inhalator	–	–	10 mg
Microtabs	2 mg	–	–

Stop smoking products

Combining different NRT products

I have known many people who have used a combination of different NRT products to suit their individual needs. This approach can be particularly helpful during the early stages of quitting where a patch is being used but the craving sensation is still 'breaking through'. In such cases, any of the five other kinds of NRT (i.e. gum, lozenge, inhalator, microtab or nasal spray) can be used to top up the nicotine level until the craving is brought under control.

At present, the manufacturers of NRT products do not advocate the multiple use of different NRT products. However, as the ultimate goal of any quit regimen is to avoid a return to the dreaded tobacco, if the need to supplement the main NRT product becomes overwhelming common sense should prevail and you may choose to consider this approach. My personal experience has shown that using a patch in combination with occasional use of nicotine gum or lozenges can be extremely useful particularly for people who are in the early stages of quitting. In fact, stop smoking advisers often give multiple NRT products for their more challenging clients in an effort to help them quit.

Cautions for NRT

When NRT first became available, various restrictions and cautions were placed on its use as part of the procedures governing the licensing of all medicines. For example, NRT products were not licensed to be used by anyone under 18 years of age, pregnant women or those with serious heart conditions. However, common sense has since prevailed and NRT products can now be legally sold or prescribed to almost any smoker who wishes to quit. In other words, if a pregnant woman or a 12-year-old child is smoking, NRT is still appropriate. We now have a more level playing field where NRT can be used without the old restrictions.

WHAT ELSE IS AVAILABLE THAT CAN HELP ME QUIT?

There are some other products available that can help a quit programme – some that we can buy over the counter and others that are available only on prescription.

If we consider that giving up is going to be a fight that we need to be determined to win, we should also think about the effects that quitting will have in the short term. There is a real possibility that we will become increasingly anxious and wary about our success, particularly during the first week after giving up tobacco. If you do become anxious, you could consider some herbal remedies to help reduce your stress and increase your ability to relax.

There are a considerable number of herbal products on the market that may help us relax and become less stressed. In particular, any products that contain passiflora, St John's wort and valerian are worth trying. At recommended doses, these should do no harm and may assist you in achieving a better state of preparedness for the challenges that lie ahead. However, although these products may reduce stress, it should be emphasised that there is no compelling scientific evidence that suggests that these types of product are effective in helping people to quit smoking in the long term. You should also be aware that certain 'herbal' medicines may interact with over-the-counter or prescription drugs that you may be taking. Therefore, please make sure you talk to your GP first if you are thinking of taking any of these products.

DRUG THERAPY FOR QUITTING

Two drugs are now available in the UK that can be prescribed by your doctor to help you quit smoking. One, Zyban®, has been available for a number of years whilst the other, Champix®, has only very recently become available in the UK.

In England and Wales, doctors follow guidelines issued by the National Institute for Health and Clinical Excellence (or NICE for short) when prescribing different drugs and treatments. NICE is an independent organisation that evaluates the clinical and cost-effectiveness of a variety of different treatments and other interventions on behalf of the NHS. NICE constantly reviews and updates its guidance and we would recommend that readers visit their website (*www.nice.org.uk*) for up-to-date information on what NICE has to say about the different drugs and treatments available to help you quit smoking.

At present, NICE guidance is only available on the use of Zyban and NRT in stopping smoking, and recommends both approaches for smokers who have expressed a desire to quit the habit. Guidance on Champix is expected to follow from NICE in 2007.

Zyban®

Zyban (generic name bupropion) is made by GlaxoSmithKline. Interestingly, its role in helping people to quit smoking was discovered purely by accident. Zyban was originally developed as an antidepressant. However, clinicians and researchers soon noticed that smokers who were given Zyban began to show less and less interest in smoking. Indeed, significant numbers of smokers began to quit altogether. This was how Zyban was introduced as a drug to treat nicotine addiction.

In essence, Zyban is a non-nicotine-based drug that appears to interrupt the action of brain chemicals which are linked to feelings of

> Drugs often have more than one name. A generic name, which refers to its active ingredient, and a brand name, which is the registered trade name given to it by the pharmaceutical company. Bupropion is a generic name and Zyban® is a brand name.

pleasure and are released when a person smokes. Consequently, it can help to reduce withdrawal symptoms and cravings for tobacco. Zyban may be particularly useful for smokers who have failed to quit using the NRT approach or who do not wish to, or cannot, use NRT. Studies that have evaluated the effectiveness of Zyban have demonstrated quit rates after 1 year of about 20%. Zyban appears to be at least as effective as NRT and in some studies was shown to be more effective at helping people quit than nicotine patches. Indeed, in practice, many thousands of smokers have successfully quit smoking using this method. There is also some evidence to show that Zyban may also be helpful for quit attempts when used in combination with NRT.

The recommended dose of Zyban is 300 mg each day, which is taken as one 150 mg tablet twice daily. Treatment with Zyban starts whilst the patient is still smoking. A target quit date is set, and treatment with Zyban starts about 2 weeks before that date whilst the patient is still smoking to give the Zyban time to start working. During the period on Zyban leading up to the quit date most smokers gradually notice less desire to smoke. Zyban therapy then continues for a further 7 to 9 weeks. An online support programme for quitting with Zyban is available at *www.thetimeisright.co.uk*.

The use of Zyban is associated with a number of side-effects including possible sleep disturbances, headache and dry mouth. In common with many other commonly used medicines, Zyban should not be used in pregnancy or by women who are breast-feeding. Remember to tell your doctor if you experience any of these side-effects. As with all medicines, it is important that you read and follow carefully the instructions set out in the patient information leaflet that can be found in the pack.

As with NRT, Zyban is more effective when you are motivated to quit smoking. Therefore, you should engage in a structured stop smoking programme with a suitably trained adviser to maximise your chances of success with this approach.

Champix®

Champix (generic name varenicline) is made by Pfizer and was only introduced into the UK in December 2006. It potentially offers a new hope for smokers who have tried and failed to quit a number of times before but yet have longed for a new treatment option to help them in their next quit attempt.

Champix is the first non-nicotine-based drug that has been developed to target and conquer the pull and draw of nicotine addiction in the brain. It works by occupying the same 'reward' space in the brain that nicotine hits, therefore blocking out some or most of the addictive effect of nicotine. This 'partial blockade' thereby reduces the craving and sense of pleasure associated with smoking.

Once the drug is taken, it works by reducing the severity of withdrawal symptoms and cravings associated with quitting. More importantly, if you do smoke after taking the drug, you get less satisfaction from smoking. In other words, it hits the same brain spot as nicotine and renders smoking pointless.

Although most of the current evidence pertaining to the use of Champix is derived from clinical trials, this experience does show that Champix is very effective at reducing withdrawal symptoms and cravings. It also appears to be very well tolerated with few side-effects and does not appear to interact with other drugs. Most importantly, levels of patient satisfaction with Champix are reported to be very high.

The Champix dosage regimen is a graduated step-up course of tablets. Before you embark on a course of treatment with Champix you need to set a quit date and the first dose of Champix should then be taken 1 to 2 weeks before this date. The idea is that Champix is given time to produce its full effect before you stop smoking so the quit attempt is much easier.

- Days 1–3, 0.5 mg is taken once daily.
- Days 4–7, 0.5 mg is taken twice daily.
- Day 8 to the end of treatment (treatment is recommended to last for 12 weeks), 1 mg is taken twice daily.
- Your target quit day should be between 8 and 14 days after starting Champix.

To give yourself the maximum chance of success from quitting smoking, please remember that Champix should always be taken in close association with, and monitored by, a trained adviser, as with Zyban and NRT.

As with all prescribed medicine, there will be a minority of patients for whom the drug is unsuitable (e.g. pregnant women and women who are breast-feeding). In clinical trials, nausea was the most common side-effect reported and this affected roughly a quarter of all people taking the drug. However, it wasn't severe enough for most to discontinue the course of treatment.

Full information about Champix is provided in the patient guidance and information leaflet included in the Champix packaging.

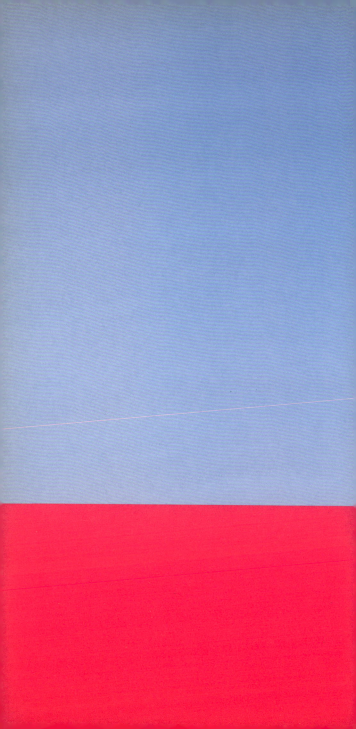

Stay stopped!

STAY STOPPED!

You've now arrived as a non-smoker! But remember, you may need ongoing help and support to make sure you stay stopped! Don't worry though. There is lots of help available!

One important fact to always remember is that once you have dumped your smoking habit you are never alone or without help! There are many helplines, websites and support materials to reinforce your determination to stay free of tobacco – why not take a look at *Simple extras* (page 108) for more information. You will also be able to access some useful materials from your counsellor who should always remain your first point of contact.

One of the most informative websites available which can give you the low-down on the facts about tobacco is *www.ash.org.uk*. This website will also link you to other sources of help and support to help you stay stopped, and treats you to some astonishing and stark facts and figures about cigarettes and tobacco. For example, did you know that 90% of all infant cot deaths occur in smokers' households?

You will probably begin to wonder why it is that civilised enlightened governments allow the manufacture, sale and distribution of any tobacco product after you learn how destructive a force it has been to the world's populations. Another interesting fact reveals that the European Union spends more on subsidising Greek tobacco farmers than it does on the entire European public health agenda. Treat yourself – find out some more facts to reinforce your determination to remain a non-smoker!

YOU'LL NOW FEEL GREAT. ENJOY THE NEW YOU!

You will find that as a smoke-free person, life will have more meaning knowing that you have a longer and happier life to live. You'll feel proud of your achievement and you will have far more money to spend. You will also smell nice – free of that stale fag smell – and begin to notice how disgusting tobacco smells are on other people. More importantly, you will begin to pity those who still smoke. You'll feel strangely superior! Enjoy yourself – you are no longer a smoker. They are the ones who now need your help to drive them away from this deadly, evil addictive curse.

TOP 20 TIPS TO HELP YOU STAY STOPPED

1. Make a list of the things on which you're going to spend your extra cash. Squashing a 20-a-day habit will yield nearly £2,000 in the first year!

2. If you're struggling from time to time, accept these feelings as part of the natural cycle of quitting. But remember... STICK TO YOUR DECISION.

3. Keep a helpline number handy for the low times. Put your favourite number on your mobile phone. These low times appear to come in 3s after quitting – 3 days, 3 weeks and 3 months – be ready for them!

4. Change your daily routine to rid yourself of the habits of the 'old you'.

5. Be careful with alcohol as drinking alcohol often goes hand in hand with smoking.

6. When cravings appear, wait for them to pass. It normally takes a minute or two for them to fade, but remember they DO fade.

7. Make four cards (the four Ds) and stick them to a noticeboard or fridge:
 - DRINK more water
 - DELAY
 - DO something else (for example, eat raw carrots, celery or fruit)
 - take DEEP breaths.

8. Keep repeating "I am a non-smoker" each day that passes and think 'smoke free'. Wake up in the morning and say to yourself "I don't smoke".

9. Put up a 'no smoking sign' in the house and use one as a screensaver on your PC.

Stay stopped!

10. Do more physical activity – take a walk, ride a bike or go for a swim.

11. Always, always refuse cigarettes when offered one and explain why to the 'dealer' – there's no such thing as an occasional fag.

12. Even better, avoid being with smokers. They will end up being your 'dealer'.

13. Thank everyone around you for their support.

14. Think about the negative aspects of smoking – smell, coughing, prolonged colds and illness, not feeling fit.

15. Change your diet – eat plenty of fresh fruit, fibre and vegetables. Build on the fantastic regeneration you are giving your body.

16. Welcome the public ban on smoking and always choose and insist on smoke-free areas when offered the choice.

17. Be proud of yourself! Give yourself a pat on the back.

18. Avoid all contact with tobacco outlets and sellers. There is no longer any need for dialogue with them – you are officially divorced!

19. When a crisis hits you, remember that reaching for a fag never solved any problems in the past and certainly didn't take the stress out of any situation.

20. Avoid doing things that you used to associate with smoking. You've arrived and there's no going back!

Stay stopped!

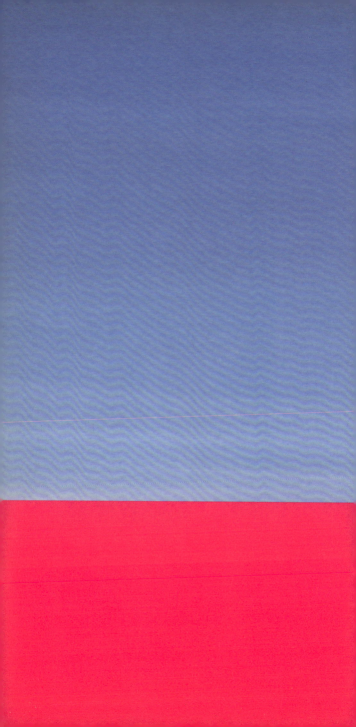

Simple extras

WHAT HAPPENS NORMALLY?

When you smoke, you are adversely affecting many processes that naturally occur in your body. Probably the two most important 'systems' that smoking affects are your respiratory system (your lungs and the 'tubes' that feed them) and your circulation (your heart and the network of capillaries, arteries and veins through which it pumps blood). To understand the damage that smoking does to these systems, it is well worth examining how these two systems work normally.

WHAT DO OUR LUNGS NORMALLY DO?

When we breathe in (inhale), air travels down our windpipe (trachea) which splits into two other tubes called bronchi thereby delivering air to each of our two lungs. Inside each lung, each bronchus divides further into smaller and smaller tubes, the smallest of which are called bronchioles. From the bronchioles, the air passes directly into tiny air sacs called alveoli. This is the part of our lungs where the exchange of carbon dioxide for oxygen takes place (see *Why is oxygen and carbon dioxide exchange important?* page 98). It is this function of the lungs that is vital to sustain life.

Simple extras

Breathing is something we don't normally think about too much and the entire process is co-ordinated subconsciously by our brain, which controls a number of 'breathing muscles' located in the ribcage. These are:

- the intercostal muscles which surround the ribs

- the diaphragm – a dome shaped muscle that separates the chest from the abdomen.

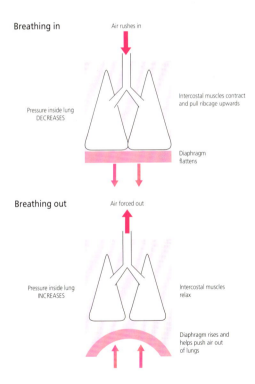

WHY IS OXYGEN AND CARBON DIOXIDE EXCHANGE IMPORTANT?

By delivering air to our bodies and exchanging carbon dioxide for oxygen, our lungs allow us to live and thrive. Without oxygen we would suffocate. This is because we need oxygen to unlock energy from food which in turn allows our body to function properly.

The surfaces of the alveoli are covered with narrow blood vessels called capillaries. Because they are so narrow, the oxygen we breathe in is passed directly from the alveoli into the bloodstream and is then pumped around our bodies by the heart (see *Your circulatory system* below). At the same time that oxygen is transferred into our bloodstream, the waste gas carbon dioxide is removed. So, the air we breathe in contains oxygen and the air we breathe out contains carbon dioxide.

YOUR CIRCULATORY SYSTEM

Your circulatory system comprises your heart and a network of arteries and veins that carry blood around your body. The arteries carry blood which has been 'oxygenated' in the lungs away from the heart towards all of the other tissues and organs in your body. Veins, on the other hand, carry 'deoxygenated' blood (from which the oxygen has been removed) back towards the heart where it is pumped to the lungs to be replenished.

The heart is the organ that is responsible for pumping blood around your body. The heart beats continuously, never pausing to rest, and ensures a continuous supply of oxygen, nutrients and other vital substances to every part of our body, allowing us to function optimally whether we are fast asleep or running a marathon. The heart is made up of four chambers which are enclosed by layers of muscle. These four chambers are called the left and right atria (singular atrium) and the left and right ventricles. During a single heart beat, the muscle of the heart contracts and the walls of these chambers are pulled in. This exerts pressure on the blood within the chambers of the heart. It is this force which pushes the blood from the atria into the ventricles and then from the ventricles out into the circulation and around the entire body.

For simplicity, the movement of blood around our bodies can be split into a number of key stages.

(1) Oxygen is transferred from the air into our bloodstream by our lungs. This oxygen-rich blood is said to be 'oxygenated'.

(2) Oxygenated blood passes into the left atrium of the heart which squeezes and pushes the blood into the left ventricle. The left ventricle has the job of pumping the oxygenated blood hard enough to reach every part of our body. It does this via the aorta (the largest artery in the body).

(3) Blood pressure in the aorta is at its highest to ensure that oxygen and other vital nutrients (like sugars, fats and vitamins) are delivered to the parts of the body that require them.

(4) The tissues and organs of the body take up the oxygen from the blood and replace it with the waste product, carbon dioxide.

(5) The blood is now 'deoxygenated' and is returned to the right atrium of the heart via the veins.

(6) The right atrium squeezes to pass the deoxygenated blood into the right ventricle which then pumps it back to the lungs where it can be replenished with fresh oxygen.

(7) The process repeats.

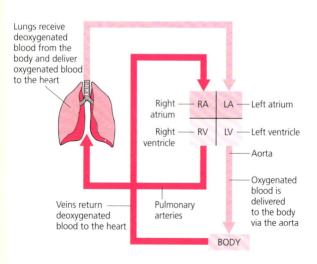

WHAT HAPPENS WHEN WE SMOKE?

When you inhale smoke from a burning cigarette it has a number of adverse effects on your lungs and your circulation (and indeed other parts of your body which we won't go into here).

In the lungs, smoking directly affects how oxygen is exchanged for carbon dioxide in the alveoli. Cigarette smoke contains many different noxious chemicals, one of which is a gas called carbon monoxide. When carbon monoxide is inhaled in the lungs it essentially reduces the blood's ability to carry oxygen. It does this because it attaches itself to haemoglobin (the red pigment in blood that carries oxygen) more easily than oxygen does. The net effect is that the amount of oxygen being delivered to the tissues of the body is substantially reduced. So, in essence, by smoking, you are gradually suffocating yourself without even being aware of it! In addition to its adverse effects on the exchange of oxygen and carbon dioxide, smoking can also obstruct and narrow the small airways of the lungs, thereby making it harder to physically deliver oxygen to the air sacs and hence to your bloodstream. Smoking also directly destroys the alveoli, which further exacerbates the effects of smoking on the exchange of oxygen for carbon dioxide in the blood.

Cigarette smoke causes the speed at which your heart pumps (i.e. your heart rate) to rise. This can put your whole circulatory system under immense pressure if it persists in the long run. Smoking is also associated with an increase in the levels of cholesterol in your blood and an increase in a number of different substances that cause your blood to clot. All of these factors can cause your arteries to 'fur up' and increase the risk of you suffering a heart attack or a stroke.

SHARED EXPERIENCES

JAMES (43)

I'd been a smoker for about 25 years when I decided to take the plunge and quit for good! Throughout this period of my life I was a 20-plus-a-day man. Looking back as a non-smoker now for the past 18 months, I can't believe that I was foolish enough to carry on for so long with a habit that I knew was slowly killing me.

Still I feel so proud of myself that I have now quit for good. It certainly wasn't easy and it took a hell of a lot of determination and, to be honest, quite a few attempts. I couldn't have done it without the support of my wife and my children and a lot of my close friends. I also made sure that I gave myself the best possible chance of quitting by using all of the services that were available to me. I went to see my GP who put me in touch with my local stop smoking service where I got loads of help and support. Not just patches and gum, but also having someone I could talk to about how to go about quitting for good.

Unfortunately, I did have to cut myself off from some of my smoking friends for a while and avoid places where I would be tempted to have a crafty fag. But looking back now, even this didn't feel like too much of a sacrifice compared with what I stood to gain from quitting. Sure, I did put on a few pounds in weight in the first few weeks, but I've now lost this from doing more exercise. I feel so much healthier now! I have so much more energy, I can taste my food again and I don't stink of stale fags. I've even met a whole new circle of friends in the badminton club I joined, and I am really pleased that some of my old smoking buddies have also quit too!

Life is just so great now! If I do have any regrets, it's that I didn't do it sooner!

MARY (34)

I admit it… I am still a smoker, although I have cut down a lot recently. I know all about the health problems probably more than most (I work for the NHS), and I really do want to quit smoking for good so I do keep trying, but I am currently stuck on between 5 and 10 cigarettes a day depending on the stress levels at work. But I will get there one day I know!

I've tried so many different methods of quitting. I guess my biggest failing is that, at the end of the day, I feel like that when I try and quit I am denying myself one of the basic pleasures in life. But I guess if I turn this on its head I am in fact denying myself a longer and healthier life. That said I am still fairly young and I feel sort of OK, though I am not exactly athletic I must admit and I do seem to get more coughs and colds than most.

I also find it hard to quit because I often find myself in the company of other smokers, particularly in pubs and clubs. Many of my smoking friends feel exactly the same way. In fact, we all can't wait for the smoking ban to come in because we all know we will find it so much easier to quit when we aren't surrounded by smoke and other smokers.

Reading this Simple Guide has really made me think again, particularly about the money side of things, so I have decided to enrol on a quit smoking programme with a couple of my friends from work. We are all determined to quit smoking for good together!

CLIFF (49)

I first started smoking when I was about 14 or 15. Thirty-five years of smoking at least 20 cigarettes a day! At today's prices that means I have quite literally set fire to more than £65,000!

Everyone smoked back then. It was just what you did. All of us teenage smokers gathered in the bike sheds during break times and over lunch, and smoked as we chatted and messed about. It felt so cool. It felt like we were all part of a big gang with a common shared interest – smoking!

In fact, I've probably felt like this for all of my adult life. I still tend to associate and socialise more with smokers than with non-smokers, particularly when I am in the pub! Unfortunately, I have lost a couple of friends fairly recently, one from a heart attack and the other had a brain tumour which they reckon started in his lungs. We all stood around in the cold at their funerals having a fag. What a bunch of idiots! We really are addicted to these things aren't we?

I have tried to quit a few times. Usually after my birthday – you know, another year older and all that – or at New Year. But I only ever seemed to be able to put up with it for a couple of days at a time. I did last a week once – went completely cold turkey! That was such a nightmare! It just made me feel so miserable and anxious. I often thought – what the hell, I'd sooner enjoy my life whilst I can and worry about the consequences later!

Well, I'll be 50 in a couple of months and I reckon now is the time to quit smoking for good! I am going to get some professional help at my local chemists. Having read this book, I quite fancy having a go at that cut down then stop approach! Wish me luck!

FURTHER READING

■ ***Simple Guides Blood Pressure***
CSF Medical Communications Ltd, 2005
ISBN: 1-905466-04-8, £5.99
www.thesimpleguides.com

USEFUL CONTACTS

■ **Action on Smoking and Health (ASH)**
Tel: 020 7739 5902
Website: *www.ash.org.uk*

■ **Asian Quitline**
Website: *www.asianquitline.org*

■ **British Heart Foundation (BHF)**
14 Fitzhardinge Street
London
W1H 6DH
Tel: 020 7935 0185
Website: *www.bhf.org.uk*
Heart information line: 08450 70 80 70

■ **CancerHelp UK (Cancer Research UK)**
Cancer Research UK
PO Box 123
Lincoln's Inn Fields
London
WC2A 3PX
Tel: 0800 226 237
Website: *www.cancerhelp.org.uk*

National Institute for Health and Clinical Excellence (NICE)
11 The Strand
London
WC2N 5HR
Tel: 020 7766 9191
Website: *www.nice.org.uk*

NHS Direct
NHS Direct Line: 0845 46 47
Website: *www.nhsdirect.nhs.uk*

NHS Smoking Helpline
Tel: 0800 169 0169 (for deaf and hard of hearing people, please use text phone 0800 169 0171)
Website: *www.gosmokefree.co.uk*

Nicorette (product information)
Website: *www.nicorette.co.uk*

Nicotinell (product information)
Website: *www.nicotinell.com*

Niquitin CQ (product information)
Website: *www.click2quit.com*

No Smoking Day
Website: *www.nosmokingday.org.uk*

QUIT
Quitline: 0800 00 22 00
Website: *www.quit.org.uk*
Email: *info@quit.org.uk*
Email advice line: *stopsmoking@quit.org.uk*

The Patients Association
PO Box 935
Harrow
Middlesex
HA1 3YJ
Helpline: 0845 6084455
Website: *www.patients-association.com*

Roy Castle Lung Cancer Foundation
200 London Road
Liverpool
Merseyside
L3 9TA
Tel: 0871 220 5426
Website: *www.roycastle.org*

The time is right
Website: *www.thetimeisright.co.uk*

YOUR RIGHTS

As a patient, you have a number of important rights. These include the right to the best possible standard of care, the right to information, the right to dignity and respect, the right to confidentiality and underpinning all of these, the right to good health.

Occasionally, you may feel as though your rights have been compromised, or you may be unsure of where you stand when it comes to qualifying for certain treatments or services. In these instances, there are a number of organisations you can turn to for help and advice. Remember that lodging a complaint against your health service should not compromise the quality of care you receive, either now or in the future.

■ The Patients Association

The Patients Association (*www.patients-association.com*) is a UK charity which represents patient rights, influences health policy and campaigns for better patient care.

Contact details:
PO Box 935
Harrow
Middlesex
HA1 3YJ
Helpline: 0845 6084455
Email: *mailbox@patients-association.com*

- **Citizens Advice Bureau**
  The Citizens Advice Bureau (*www.nacab.org.uk*) provides free, independent and confidential advice to NHS patients at a number of outreach centres located throughout the country (*www.adviceguide.org.uk*).
  Contact details:
  Find your local Citizens Advice Bureau using the search tool at *www.citizensadvice.org.uk*.

- **Patient Advice and Liaison Services (PALS)**
  Set up by the Department of Health (*www.dh.gov.uk*), PALS provide information, support and confidential advice to patients, families and their carers.
  Contact details:
  Phone your local hospital, clinic, GP surgery or health centre and ask for details of the PALS, or call NHS Direct on 0845 46 47.

- **The Independent Complaints Advocacy Service (ICAS)**
  ICAS is an independent service that can help you bring about formal complaints against your NHS practitioner. ICAS provides support, help, advice and advocacy from experienced advisers and caseworkers.
  Contact details:
  ICAS Central Team
  Myddelton House
  115–123 Pentonville Road
  London N1 9LZ
  Email: *icascentralteam@citizensadvice.org.uk*
  Or contact your local ICAS office direct.

Accessing your medical records

You have a legal right to see all your health records under the Data Protection Act of 1998. You can usually make an informal request to your doctor and you should be given access within 40 days. Note that you may have to pay a small fee for the privilege.

You can be denied access to your records if your doctor believes that the information contained within them could cause serious harm to you or another person. If you are applying for access on behalf of someone else, then you will not be granted access to information which the patient gave to his or her doctor on the understanding that it would remain confidential.

NOTES

SIMPLE GUIDES QUESTIONNAIRE

Dear Reader,

We would love to know what you thought of this Simple Guide. Please take a few moments to fill out this short questionnaire and return it to us at the FREEPOST address below.

Freepost RRKL-ZTHH-XYJZ
CSF Medical Communications Ltd
Eagle Tower, Montpellier Drive, Cheltenham, GL50 1TA

SO WHAT DID YOU THINK?

Which Simple Guide have you just read?

_____

Where did you buy it (store/town)?

_____

Who did you buy it for?

- ☐ Myself
- ☐ Patient
- ☐ Friend
- ☐ Other
- ☐ Relative

Where did you hear about the Simple Guides?

- ☐ They were recommended to me
- ☐ Stumbled across them
- ☐ Internet
- ☐ Other

Did it meet with your expectations?

- ☐ Exceeded
- ☐ Met most
- ☐ Met all
- ☐ Fell below

Was there anything you particularly liked?

_____

_____

_____

Was there anything we could have improved?

_____

_____

_____

WHO ARE YOU?

Name: _____

Address: _____

_____

_____

Tel: _____

Email: _____

How old are you?

☐ Under 25 ☐ 25–34 ☐ 35–44
☐ 45–54   ☐ 55–64 ☐ 65+

Are you...   ☐ Male   ☐ Female

Do you suffer from a long-term medical condition? If so, please specify.

_____

WHAT NEXT?

What other topics would you like to see covered in future Simple Guides?

Thanks,
   the Simple Guides team